JASON, the ARGONAUTS, and the GOLDEN FLEECE

AN INTERACTIVE MYTHOLOGICAL ADVENTURE

by Blake Hoena

illustrated by Nadine Takvorian & James Nathan

Consultant: Dr. Laurel Bowman
Department of Greek and Roman Studies
University of Victoria
Victoria, BC, Canada

CAPSTONE PRESS
a capstone imprint

You Choose Books are published by Capstone Press,
1710 Roe Crest Drive, North Mankato, Minnesota 56003
www.mycapstone.com

Library of Congress Cataloging-in-Publication Data
Cataloging-in-Publication Data is on file with the Library of Congress.
ISBN 978-1-4914-8113-4 (library binding)
ISBN 978-1-4914-8118-9 (paperback)
ISBN 978-1-4914-8120-2 (eBook PDF)

Editorial Credits
Michelle Hasselius, editor; Russell Griesmer, designer;
Wanda Winch, media researcher; Kathy McColley, production specialist

Image Credits
Shutterstock: Alex Novikov, paper scroll, Eky Studio,
old stone wall, reyhan, piece of stone, Samira Dragonfly, Baroque frame,
Tymokno Galyna, Greek columns

Printed and bound in Canada.
009632F16

Table of Contents

About Your Adventure

YOU are the mighty Greek hero Jason. Along with your crew of Argonauts, you set sail on your quest for the legendary Golden Fleece. On your way, you will face deadly monsters, mythical beasts, and dangerous gods. Can you survive and claim your reward?

Chapter One sets the scene. Then you choose which path to take. Follow the directions at the bottom of each page. The choices you make determine what happens next. After you finish your path, go back and read the others for more adventures.

YOU CHOOSE the path you take through this mythical adventure.

CHAPTER 1

The Man With One Sandal

You stand atop Mount Pelion. Off in the distance you see the city of Iolcus. It was once your home.

"Jason!" a voice calls from behind you. You turn to see a half-man, half-horse creature waving to you. It's your mentor, Chiron. You were placed in the old centaur's care as an infant after the death of your father, King Aeson. He showed you how to fight and taught you how to heal yourself and others. He even told you how your father had been killed. Your uncle Pelias had overthrown him as ruler of Iolcus.

Turn the page.

Now that you've reached adulthood, you've decided it is time for you to return to Iolcus. You plan to reclaim the throne that had once belonged to your father.

"Always be kind to those you meet," Chiron says. You nod and then turn to your destination.

You begin the long hike down Mount Pelion. Upon reaching the foothills at the base of the mountain, you hear the rush of water. A river blocks your path. As you walk toward its bank, you see a woman dressed in rags. She is sitting on a fallen log near the water.

"Could you help me, young man?" she asks. "I need to get across."

Her hand shakes as she reaches for you. You help her stand. She's old and frail. She grabs your arm to steady herself.

You turn from her to the river. Its current is swift. You doubt she could cross it on her own. You think about Chiron's words: *Always be kind to those you meet.*

You pick up the old woman and lift her onto your back. She's as light as a feather. You fear a strong gust of wind could carry her away. She'll be easy to carry.

The water splashes as you take your first steps into the river. After a few more steps, you notice something odd. The old woman isn't so light anymore. Her weight starts to press down on you. With each step, she grows heavier. Your back begins to ache. Your knees wobble. Your feet sink into the muddy river bottom. You start to worry that you might not make it to the other side.

Turn the page.

As you walk, one of your sandals slips off your foot. But you can't pick it up. You can barely place one foot in front of the next.

Upon reaching the opposite shore, you set the woman down. Then you collapse, exhausted. You look up but she is gone, nowhere to be seen.

Where did she go? you wonder.

Even though you wear only one sandal, you begin the long walk to Iolcus. When you reach the city's main gate, you are disappointed. The stories Chiron told you about Iolcus described it as a wealthy city. But now it is rundown. Garbage litters the streets.

Iolcus' citizens walk with their heads hung low, until they see you. People stop and stare as you walk by. They talk excitedly and point at your feet.

"He has just one sandal," one man says.

"It's the prophecy," a woman gasps.

You walk up to a nearby group of people. "What prophecy?" you ask.

An elderly woman explains, "An oracle said that a man wearing one sandal would come and take the throne from King Pelias."

You are about to ask another question when three city guards surround you. They take you to a palace in the center of the city. You are brought to the throne room, where King Pelias greets you.

"It's good to see you, nephew," King Pelias says, smiling. "I've been waiting for your return. Do you wish to sit on your father's throne?"

You nod, but Pelias quickly leads you to a window overlooking the city.

Turn the page.

"Iolcus was once a wealthy city," Pelias says. "Its people will want a ruler able to bring the city to its former glory."

"How can I do that?" you ask.

"The Golden Fleece," he says. "It is a priceless treasure found in Colchis. Seek it out and bring it back to Iolcus. With the Golden Fleece, you'll be able to return Iolcus to what it once was and prove that you are worthy of being the king.

With the Golden Fleece, Pelias could not deny you as ruler of Iolcus. But it will be a quest with many dangers. Which one will you face first?

To face Harpies and sail past the Cyanean Rocks,
turn to page 15.

To tame fire-breathing bulls and battle a dragon,
turn to page 45.

To face Scylla and Charybdis, turn to page 81.

CHAPTER 2

King Phineus and the Harpies

As you leave the palace, a woman walks up. She is tall and proud. You realize she is Athena, goddess of wisdom and protector of heroes.

"Jason, I've been sent to help you," Athena says.

"By whom?" you ask.

"The goddess Hera herself," Athena says. "She told me to find a sturdy craft for your quest. Hera has put out a call for the world's greatest heroes to join you. Zetes and Calais have agreed. They are the sons of Boreas, god of the north wind. They have wings on their ankles and can fly."

Turn the page.

"Why would Hera help me?" you ask.

"The old woman you helped cross the river was actually Hera in disguise," Athena says. "She was testing you to see if you were worthy of her help."

Athena walks you down to the city docks. There she introduces you to Argus, a shipbuilder.

"Nice to meet you, mate," he says. Then Argus and Athena discuss the ship you will need for your quest.

Weeks later, you have a mighty ship. It is called the Argo, named after the man who built it.

As Athena promised, heroes have begun showing up to join your crew. They will be known as the Argonauts.

In all, 50 heroes join you. Like Zetes and Calais, some are the descendants of gods. Ancaeus is a son of the sea god Poseidon. Other heroes are the sons of kings, such as Acastus, King Pelias' own son.

Finally you are ready to set sail. You leave to great fanfare. Rumors of your quest have spread throughout Iolcus. Nearly everyone in the city is at the docks to see you off, even your old mentor, Chiron.

Each of the heroes who joined you takes a seat at the oars. They bend their backs and then pull. The Argo lurches forward into the calm sea.

As you sail away, you see Chiron on the beach waving to you. "God speed and a safe journey!" he calls out.

Turn the page.

After being at sea for some time, you come across an island. Ancaeus tells you that it's the home of King Phineus.

"Some say he is a seer," Ancaeus says. "Perhaps he could help guide us on our quest."

"I hear he has been cursed by Zeus," Acastus says, "for revealing the secrets of men's futures."

"I have heard that too," Ancaeus agrees. "He has been plagued by Harpies."

A seer like King Phineus could warn you of the dangers you might face on your journey. But you are worried about facing the Harpies. They are known to be extremely mean and dangerous. These half-women, half-bird creatures have razor-sharp talons that can rip men to shreds.

To help King Phineus, go to page 19.

To avoid the Harpies, turn to page 22.

You set anchor and go ashore with Zetes and Calais. The sons of Boreas can fly. Who better to help you face the Harpies?

As you approach Phineus' palace, you notice it is in shambles. The grounds have not been tended. Weeds and thistles grow everywhere. Stones are crumbling from the walls, and there are several holes in the roof.

No servants greet you at the front door, so you walk in. The inside of the palace looks even worse than the outside. Garbage litters the floor, and torn tapestries hang from the walls. The stench of filth fills the air.

Turn the page.

As you enter the throne room, the smell grows stronger. The mess is even worse here. The walls and floor are covered with rotten food. An old man sits on the throne. He leans forward with his head in his hands. He is so thin, his skin hangs from his bones. You would think he was dead if he didn't let out a deep sigh.

"King Phineus?" you ask.

The old man looks up. "Have you brought me my dinner?" he asks.

You and your men step fully into the room. "No sire, we haven't," you reply.

"No matter," the king says. "Those Harpies would just snatch it away." He points up at the roof to the holes you saw outside.

"What of the Harpies?" you ask.

"The Harpies have scared away most of my servants," he says. "And even worse, any time a plate of food is set in front of me, they swoop down and steal my meal before I can get a bite."

Phineus points at the heaps of rotten food on the floor. "Whatever food they don't take is too foul to eat," he continues. "If you rid me of the Harpies, I will tell you of the dangers that lie ahead on your journey."

To kill the Harpies, turn to page 24.

To chase the Harpies away, turn to page 29.

You decide not to stop and help King Phineus. He may have been able to tell you of the dangers you will face on your quest. But you worry about angering Zeus, ruler of the gods. You do not want to risk his wrath and be cursed too. So you sail past King Phineus' island.

After a few more days of sailing, you come upon a narrow strait. Both sides of the channel are lined with towering cliffs. You search them for signs of danger but see none.

"I believe those are the Cyanean Rocks," Ancaeus says.

"Do you know what dangers lie ahead?" you ask.

"No," Ancaeus replies. "But there is danger behind us. A storm is brewing. We'll need to seek shelter."

You turn to see a darkening sky. Lightning dances along the horizon, and you hear the distant rumble of thunder.

You have two choices. You could sail through the strait, where the Cyanean Rocks would protect you from the brunt of the storm. Or you could anchor near shore to ride the storm out. You wouldn't risk sailing through the strait and into unknown dangers. But the Argo would be more open to the storm near shore.

To sail through the Cyanean Rocks, turn to page 32.

To anchor near shore and wait out the storm, turn to page 35.

With Zetes and Calais, you plot to kill the Harpies. It will be tricky, as the Harpies can fly away from you. But Zetes and Calais can fly too.

First you need to lure the Harpies into the throne room. You deliver Phineus' next meal. It's a heaping plate of roast lamb, cheese, olives, and figs with honey. The king looks at it longingly, as if he hasn't eaten a decent meal in years. And he hasn't.

Before the king can pick up his knife and fork, you hear a deafening screech from above. Two Harpies swoop down through holes in the roof. One dives toward the king, causing him to duck under the table. The other snatches up the plate of food, spilling only crumbs onto the floor. The Harpies cackle and shriek as they begin to fly away.

Turn the page.

But Zetes and Calais hover in the air, blocking the holes that the Harpies flew through. They are armed with spears. The Harpies hiss. Then they spin around and fly back toward you. From underneath Phineus' table, you pull out a spear that you have hidden.

The Harpies screech and dart toward a nearby window. But you have prepared for this too. On your command, all the windows and doors are filled with your men. They are armed with bows and have arrows nocked. They let the arrows loose, and the Harpies cry in pain as they are struck down.

That night Phineus has a feast in your honor. His tables are laden with all sorts of meats, vegetables and fruits, and desserts. You and your men stuff yourselves as Phineus tells you of the dangers you will face and how best to avoid them.

The next morning you and your men walk out to the Argo. Phineus joins you. "I wish you the best of luck," he says.

You are about to respond when one of your men shouts, "What is that?"

A single black cloud floats overhead. Once it is above the Argo, a flash of lightning strikes your ship. BOOM! The following thunderclap is deafening. Your ship bursts into flames.

Turn the page.

"Look!" shouts one of your men. Flying toward you is an entire flock of Harpies.

"There are too many to fight!" you cry. "Go back to Phineus' palace!"

"I fear you angered Zeus by killing his Harpies," Phineus says. "He has cursed you to suffer the same fate as me."

It's true. Any time you or one of your men tries to eat a bite of food, one of the many Harpies swoops down and steals it.

Soon you are so hungry, you forget about your quest or of becoming Iolcus' king. All you want is one small mouthful of food. But the Harpies keep denying you until you waste away and die from extreme hunger.

THE END

To follow another path, turn to page 13.

To learn more about Jason, turn to page 103.

With Zetes and Calais, you plan a way to chase away the Harpies. With their ability to fly, you figure Zetes and Calais will be best for the task.

You deliver Phineus' next meal. The king looks at the food longingly, as if he hasn't eaten a decent meal in years. As soon as you set the plate down, you hear the flap of wings overhead. You look up to see two Harpies dive through the holes in the roof. They screech and hiss. You step back as one swoops down at Phineus, causing the king to duck under the table. The other snatches up his meal in her talons.

"Zetes! Calais!" you shout. "After them!"

With spears in hand, the brothers launch into the air. The Harpies shriek as they dart through holes in the ceiling.

Turn the page.

Zetes and Calais keep after the Harpies until the goddess Iris appears before them. She asks them to stop. Iris worries that if the brothers kill the Harpies, Zeus will curse Jason and his crew. The goddess promises that she won't let the Harpies bother King Phineus again.

That night Phineus holds a feast in your honor. The tables are piled high with food. Your men eat, drink, and celebrate with the king. During your meal, Phineus tells of the dangers ahead.

" ... and then," Phineus warns, "you will come across the Cyanean Rocks. They rise up on both sides of a narrow strait. Whenever a ship sails through the channel, the rocks crash together and destroy it."

"Then how will we get through?" you ask.

Phineus asks one of his servants to bring you a cage with a white dove. "Let this dove fly through first," Phineus explains. "After the rocks crash together, they slowly drift apart. Have your men put their backs into their oars and row as fast as they can."

You thank the king and set sail the next morning. Before long you come upon the Cyanean Rocks. You do as Phineus said. You let the dove fly between the cliffs first. Just as Phineus predicted, the cliffs crash together. BOOM! The bird narrowly escapes being crushed to death.

Then as the rocks drift apart, your men row as fast as they can. The Argo slips through the strait just as the rocks come crashing together again.

Turn to page 38.

"Let's go toward the shelter of those cliffs," you command.

Your men grasp their oars and pull with all their might. The Argo lurches forward.

Then the winds pick up and the rain begins to beat down. But your men keep rowing, and the Argo makes it into the strait as the worst of the storm hits. The weather is much calmer between the towering cliffs.

But then one of your men shouts, "Look at the walls! They are moving!"

"Back! Back!" you shout.

Between the moving walls and your orders, the men are confused. Some row backwards, some forward, and others not at all. The Argo stops dead in the water as the rocks close in.

Turn the page.

Men wedge their oars between the moving cliff walls, but the wooden oars snap almost instantly. Then the walls bump up against the ship's haul. You hear popping and snapping as the deck buckles and railings shatter.

As the rock walls keep closing in, the Argo simply disintegrates under your feet. You plunge into the water as the walls close in, crushing everything between them. They smash together with an echoing BOOM! Then they slowly drift apart. All that remains of the Argo and the Argonauts are splintered pieces of driftwood.

THE END

To follow another path, turn to page 13.

To learn more about Jason, turn to page 103.

Not wanting to risk sailing into unknown waters, you decide to anchor your ship near shore. Then the storm hits. The wind tears at your sails. Rain pelts your ship. Large waves crash into the side of the ship, drenching you and your men.

You shout orders, "Tie up the sails! Pull in the oars!"

Over the sound of the crashing waves and thunderclaps, you hear a loud BOOM! "What was that?" you ask the nearest man.

"Look!" he points toward the narrow strait. The cliff walls seem closer together now. "Just watch," the man says.

You see a piece of driftwood float into the strait. Then suddenly, BOOM! The cliff walls smash together, crushing everything between them.

Turn the page.

You are thankful that you chose to anchor your ship rather than sail through the strait. The next morning, you have a plan. You have your men row the Argo out in front of the opening through the strait.

"We can't sail through that," one of your men says.

"Didn't you see what happened last night?" another asks. "We'll be crushed."

"Just be ready for my order," you say as confidently as you can.

You stand at the ship's stern and search the water. Your men wait impatiently. Then you see a large piece of driftwood bobbing along the current. It floats by the Argo and into the strait.

"Put your backs into it and row!" you order.

In front of you the towering cliffs smash together, demolishing the piece of driftwood. Then they begin to slowly drift apart.

The Argo slips between the towering cliffs. They are still close enough that some of your oars scrape against them.

You can see the worried looks on your men, but it's too late to turn back now. So you urge them on. The ship leaps forward as it picks up speed.

Just as the rocks stop moving apart, the Argo exits the other side of the strait. BOOM! The rocks crash together again right behind you, but you are safely away.

Turn to page 38.

After passing through the Cyanean Rocks, you continue on. Then one day an Argonaut points to a large bird flying overhead. The sun glints off of it as if the bird is metallic.

"What is it? Do you know?" you ask. Everyone shakes his head no.

You notice more birds. They dot the sky. Then one of the birds swoops down toward your ship. As it flies overhead, you hear a TINK! TINK! TINK! Three metallic feathers are at your feet, stuck in the deck.

It attacked us! you think. Another bird begins to dive, and then another, and another. Soon metal feathers are raining down on you and the Argonauts.

To fend off the birds, turn to page 40.

To flee from the birds, turn to page 42.

"Shields up!" you command. The crew quickly drops their oars and grabs their shields.

Metal feathers thud into the wooden deck. They clink off the Argonauts' shields. Every now and then, a man screams as a feather strikes him.

You aren't sure what to do. The flock of birds surrounds the Argo. Most of your men are hiding under the cover of their shields. Some have drawn their swords and are swinging at the birds, which stay just out of reach.

Then you notice that as one of the men swings his sword, he accidently hits it against his shield. CLANG! The birds near him shriek and fly off.

That gives you an idea. You pick up a club and bang it against your shield. CLANG! CLANG! The birds around you shriek and fly away.

"Do as I do!" you shout to the crew.

You clang on your shield some more. Your men grab swords and clubs to beat on their shields. The sound is deafening, but it does the trick. The birds are driven off.

"To the oars!" you shout. "We want to be away from here in case they come back."

Your crew jumps to obey. The Argo lurches forward, and soon you are safely away from danger. You and the Argonauts have survived the first part of your quest to find the Golden Fleece.

THE END

To follow another path, turn to page 13.

To learn more about Jason, turn to page 103.

"Row!" you shout to the Argonauts. "Put your backs into it."

You hope to escape the flock of deadly birds. But shouts ring out as some of the men are struck by metal feathers. You order some of the Argonauts to hold up their shields to protect the men at the oars.

You call Calais and Zetes over to you. "Do you think you can chase them off?" you ask.

"We can try," the brothers answer as they launch into the air.

Calais and Zetes attack the birds with spears. They even knock a couple out of the air. But then the birds attack. They have bronze beaks and sharp talons. You watch in horror as the birds swarm around Calais and Zetes. The brothers are torn apart.

"Archers!" you call. Half a dozen men join at the front of the ship. "See if you can shoot them down," you yell.

Arrows fly through the air. Most bounce off the metallic birds. Then the birds swoop over head and sharp metal feathers rain down on your archers, killing them. The birds do not stop their attack until you and all of the Argonauts are dead. Then they land on the Argo and start to eat.

THE END

To follow another path, turn to page 13.

To learn more about Jason, turn to page 103.

CHAPTER 3

The King and the Witch

As you leave the palace, a woman walks up to you. She is tall and proud, and you recognize her instantly. She is Athena, the goddess of wisdom and protector of heroes.

"Jason," Athena calls to you. "Hera has sent me to help you."

"I'd be grateful for any help you offer," you say, bowing to the goddess. "But why would Hera want to help me?"

Then you remember the old lady you helped on your way to Iolcus. She just disappeared after you crossed the river. That must have been Hera in disguise.

Turn the page.

"A local shipbuilder named Argus will build you a ship worthy of your quest," says Athena. "Hera has also called forth heroes from across the land to join you."

You can hardly believe your good fortune. In a matter of weeks, you have a ship, the Argo, and a crew of heroes called the Argonauts to man its oars.

Your journey from Iolcus is filled with danger, but you and the Argonauts eventually reach Colchis. As your crew ties your ship up at the docks, a group of soldiers from the city guard marches up to you.

"I am Jason of Iolcus," you say.

"King Aeetes wishes to know why you have come to our city," the commander of the soldiers says.

"We are here on a quest to find the Golden Fleece," you proudly say.

"Then King Aeetes will want to see you," the commander says with a sneer. "Until then, you must stay aboard your ship."

To enforce his order, the commander stations guards at the end of the dock. Then he departs.

To wait for King Aeetes, turn to page 48.

To seek the Golden Fleece alone, turn to page 50.

The next day the guard commander returns with more soldiers. "Come with us," he says.

You take the Argonauts Argus, Phrontis, Melas, and Cytisorus with you. As you leave the ship, guards surround you. They lead you to the king's palace.

King Aeetes greets you in the throne room. "I hear you have come for the Golden Fleece," he says with a smile. "Why?"

You explain what happened to your father and Iolcus, and the quest that your uncle Pelias sent you on. You even tell him of the dangers you faced to reach his shores.

"Yours seems like a worthy quest," the king says. "But you are not the only hero who has asked for me for the Golden Fleece." Suddenly the king's smile turns sinister. "To prove you are worthy of such a prize, I have a task you must first complete."

By the look the king gives you, you worry it will be an impossible task.

"What is it, sire?" you ask.

"I only ask that you hook my prized bulls to a plow and sow my field with these dragon's teeth," King Aeetes says. He holds up a sack for you to see.

To accept the task, turn to page 53.

To refuse the task, turn to page 55.

That night as everyone sleeps, you quietly leave your ship. You plan to sneak into the palace. The Golden Fleece has to be there. You could only bring a dagger as a weapon, so you hope you don't run into any trouble.

But as you approach the palace, you see a dull, golden light upon the horizon. You head over in the light's direction. You find yourself at the foot of a hill. Atop it is an old, twisted tree bare of leaves. The Golden Fleece is draped over its lowest branch.

You are about to walk up the hill when a female voice stops you. "I wouldn't do that if I were you," she warns.

In the dark, you can't quite make out who the speaker is. But she seems young, about your age.

Turn the page.

You look closer at the tree. In the shadows under the tree's branches, you see something snakelike move.

"A giant serpent?" you ask.

"It is the dragon that never sleeps," the voice says.

"Then how can I get the Golden Fleece?" you ask.

"You can't," she says. "Not even my father dares go near it with the dragon on guard." Then you realize whom you are speaking to: King Aeetes' daughter.

To take the princess captive, turn to page 57.

To run away from the princess, turn to page 59.

The task seems simple enough. Chiron taught you to farm, so you accept.

"Then return here tomorrow to do as you've been asked," the king says.

You and your men turn to leave the palace. As you walk out of the throne room, a young woman walks by you. Your eyes meet. At first she sneers at you. But then suddenly her look changes, as if she were struck by one of Eros' arrows. She smiles and blushes as you and your men leave.

"That was Medea, the king's daughter," one of your crew whispers. "I hear she's a witch."

Back on your ship, you tell the Argonauts about the task the king has set forth for you. They laugh and joke, thinking it's funny that one of the world's greatest heroes has been reduced to farm work.

Turn the page.

The next day guards come for you. You leave with them, bringing Argus, Phrontis, Melas, and Cytisorus along with you.

As the guards lead you toward the palace, a robed woman steps out from a crowd of people and bumps into you. You recognize Medea immediately.

"Take this," she whispers, tucking a bottle into your hand. "Cover yourself from head to toe if you wish to survive." Then she ducks back into the crowd.

To throw the bottle away, turn to page 62.

To trust Medea, turn to page 64.

You laugh at the king's offer. "I lead a crew of some of the world's greatest heroes," you say. "I shouldn't have to farm your land. I should be fighting monsters!"

The king laughs at your bragging. "Very well," he says. "I have a dragon for you to battle."

Guards surround you and your men. You are led outside to a hill. Atop the hill is a gnarled old tree, and hanging from its lowest branches shines a golden object.

"It's the fleece!" you say, turning to your men.

But their looks of amazement quickly turn to fear. Looking back at the Golden Fleece, you see why. A dragon is curled around the base of the tree. It stirs and hisses.

Turn the page.

"Well, go on," the king says.

His guards prod you forward with their spears. You have no other choice but to face the dragon. You and your men draw your swords as the dragon strikes. Its attack is quick and vicious, and your swords don't even scratch its scaly body. As the dragon grabs you in its jaws to end your life, you swear you hear the king laughing.

THE END

To follow another path, turn to page 13.

To learn more about Jason, turn to page 103.

It occurs to you that you could use the princess to your advantage. You could take her captive and use her as a hostage. Then the king would have to give you the Golden Fleece. You draw your dagger and take a step toward the princess.

"What are you doing?" she asks, backing away.

"I'm taking you with me," you say. You grab the princess' wrist.

She does not fight or pull away. She only smiles. There's something about her grin that scares you, as if she knows something you do not.

"You have not heard of me, have you?" she asks.

Turn the page.

"No," you say. "I don't even know your name."

"It's Medea," the princess replies, "the witch daughter of King Aeetes."

Suddenly vines shoot up from the ground. They wrap tightly around you, binding your legs and arms. Before you can scream for help, they wrap around your throat and choke you to death.

THE END

To follow another path, turn to page 13.

To learn more about Jason, turn to page 103.

You worry that the princess will call for help, so you turn to run.

"Wait," she calls after you. You stop and look back. "My name is Medea," she says. "And my father, King Aeetes, will offer you a challenge tomorrow. Accept it."

"Why are you helping me?" you ask.

Medea steps toward you close enough so that you can see her face. She looks at you lovingly. "I'm not sure," she says. "It's as if Eros stuck me with one of his arrows, and I …" Her voices trails off, and she blushes.

You aren't sure what to say, so you thank her. You head back toward your ship. You tell your crew about your encounter with Medea and what you expect will happen tomorrow.

Turn the page.

"I've heard she's a witch," one of your men says.

"Can you trust her?" another asks.

"I hope so," you reply.

The next morning you are taken to King Aeetes' court. Medea stands next to her father and gives you a nod of recognition. As Medea said, the king offers you a challenge. He asks you to plow his field with his bulls, and then sow the field with dragon's teeth. If you succeed, the king says he will give you the Golden Fleece.

It seems like an odd challenge. But among the many things Chiron taught you, one of them was how to farm. You happily accept. Afterward you are taken back to your ship to wait and prepare for your task.

The next day, guards come for you. You leave with them, bringing Argus, Phrontis, Melas, and Cytisorus along with you. As the guards lead you toward the palace, a robed woman steps out from a crowd of people and bumps into you. You recognize Medea immediately.

"Take this," she says, placing a bottle into your hand. "Cover yourself from head to toe if you wish to survive." Then she ducks back into the crowd.

To ignore Medea, go to page 62.

To trust Medea, turn to page 64.

Medea is the king's daughter and a witch. You just can't trust her, even if she seems helpful. The bottle she handed you could be poison. As you're walking, you toss it aside into some bushes.

The guards lead you to a large field. King Aeetes is waiting. Medea stands beside her father. A wooden yoke is placed at your feet. Then the king points to a pen at the far end of the field.

"And there are my prized bulls," he says.

Not only are the bulls huge, but you swear smoke curls out of their nostrils. You carry the yoke to the pen, then open its gate and step in. The bulls charge at you as fire shoots from their nostrils. While you are able to avoid their horns, you can't escape their deadly, fiery breath.

THE END

To follow another path, turn to page 13.

To learn more about Jason, turn to page 103.

You aren't sure why the king's daughter would offer to help you. At first you think it might be some sort of trick. But then you begin to worry about the task at hand. Why would the king offer to give you the Golden Fleece for doing something as simple as plowing a field and planting some dragon's teeth? You decide to do as Medea said. As you walk with the guards, you pour the contents of the bottle into your hands and start rubbing it on your arms and legs.

The guards take you to a large field, where the king and his court wait for you. Medea stands next to her father. At one end of the field is a pen.

"And there are my prized bulls," the king says.

You walk over to the pen. The bulls are large and muscular, and smoke curls from their nostrils as they breathe.

Turn the page.

You leap into the pen with the yoke. The bulls charge, and fire shoots from their nostrils. Flames dance around your feet as you grab one bull by the horns. But the fire does not burn you. Then you realize Medea's potion is protecting you from the fire. You put the yoke on one bull, and then slip it on the other bull when it charges you.

Once you are ready, a guard opens the pen's gate, and you lead the bulls out. You hook up the plow and begin the first part of your task. You lead them back and forth across the field. The plow digs into the earth, creating deep furrows. Out of the corner of your eye, you see the king angrily watching.

When you are done, the guards lead the bulls away. You go to stand before the king. "I have plowed your field," you say defiantly.

Turn the page.

The king holds up a small sack and says, "You have yet to sow these dragon's teeth."

You grab the sack from him, reach into it, and pull out a handful of teeth. You throw them into the furrows. As soon as the teeth hit the ground, they start to grow. But it's not plants that sprout from them. It is men—men made of dirt. They carry shields and swords as they rise up from the ground.

To grab a spear to fight the earthmen,
go to page 67.

To pick up a boulder to throw at the earthmen,
turn to page 68.

As the earthmen rise up from the ground, you say, "Give me a shield and spear."

You strap the shield to one arm and then lower the spear at the earthmen. They outnumber you, but your spear is longer than their swords. That gives you the advantage.

Then the earthmen turn to attack. You lunge at the first earthman. Your spear plunges into his stomach. But it doesn't stop him. The spear just goes right through the earthman. He advances toward you with the spear still stuck in his belly. You deflect his sword strike with your shield. But you aren't as lucky when the rest of the earthmen surround you. You are now weaponless. As they stab and slice at you, you can't defend against their many attacks.

THE END

To follow another path, turn to page 13.

To learn more about Jason, turn to page 103.

The earthmen outnumber you. But off to the side of the field, you see a large boulder. You pick it up over your head. With a mighty heave, you toss it into the middle of the earthmen. The huge rock knocks some of them over and crushes others rising from the ground.

But what happens next is unexpected. The rock angers and confuses the earthmen. Instead of turning to attack you, they turn on each other. During the confusion, you sneak up on them. You pick up a sword dropped by one of the fallen earthmen. You hack and slash at the earthmen rising up from the ground.

Then one of the earthmen swings its sword at you. You duck and strike at its legs. He falls to the ground and breaks apart. Then another earthman strikes. You slice off his sword arm and then his head. The earthman crumbles.

Turn the page.

In a wild fury, you attack the rest of the earthmen. While you are still outnumbered, your sword easily slices through their earthen bodies, causing them to crumble apart. The fight is over quickly. All that's left of the earthmen are piles of dirt.

Then you turn to King Aeetes, who simply glares at you. "Give me the Golden Fleece as you promised," you demand.

"First you must rest after your trials," the king says. "I will send for you tomorrow after I retrieve the Golden Fleece."

To go get the fleece yourself,
go to page 71.

To trust that King Aeetes will give you the fleece,
turn to page 72.

You are suspicious that the king doesn't give you the fleece right away. And you see the questioning look Medea gives her father.

That night you look for the fleece yourself. You think the king must keep it in the palace. As you creep through the night, you see a golden glow coming from a hilltop not far away.

It's the Golden Fleece, you think.

An old, gnarled tree stands on top of the hill. The Golden Fleece hangs from one of its lowest branches. You rush up the hill. As you reach the top, a large shadow stirs at the base of the tree. You hear a hiss. The shadow rises up above you. It is long and snakelike. A dragon! It strikes with deadly quickness, killing you instantly.

THE END

To follow another path, turn to page 13.

To learn more about Jason, turn to page 103.

You are not happy that the king didn't bring the fleece with him. But it is valuable. It makes sense that he would have to retrieve the fleece from its hiding place.

You and your crew go back to your ship to wait. Just as the sun is setting, one of your men knocks on your cabin door. "There is someone here to see you," he says.

You head up to the deck, and there stands Medea covered in a large robe. "I had to sneak out of the palace," she says, looking up at you. You see that there are tears in her eyes.

"What is it?" you ask, taking a step closer to her.

"My father isn't going to give you the fleece," she says. "He plans to kill you and your men."

"When?" you ask.

"Tonight while you sleep," Medea answers.

"Then we will fight," you say.

"His army is too great for your Argonauts to defeat," she says. "You must leave."

"But not without the fleece," you say.

Medea looks down and sighs, as if she's thinking something through. Then after a moment, she looks up at you. "I will help you retrieve the fleece if you promise me one thing," she says.

"What? Anything," you say.

"Take me away with you," she says, "and agree to marry me."

To accept Medea's offer, turn to page 74.
To say no to Medea's offer, turn to page 75.

Medea has already done so much to help you. But marry her? You aren't sure. But you are asking her to help you take her father's most valued treasure.

She smiles and gives you a hug when you say yes. Then she takes your hand.

She leads you down the docks. You are surprised that the guards don't stop you. But then you see that they are asleep and snoring loudly.

Medea leads you to a hilltop where the Golden Fleece hangs from a gnarled, old tree. At the base of the tree, you see a dark shadow move. As it unwinds itself from the tree's trunk, it slithers toward you. "My father picked this dragon to guard the fleece because it never sleeps," Medea says.

To fight the dragon, turn to page 77.

To ask Medea to cast a spell, turn to page 78.

Even though Medea helped you get this far, she asks too much. What would the people of Iolcus think if you brought home a wife who is a witch? "I'm sorry," you tell her.

Your refusal angers her. "You will have stay here with me forever!" she screams.

Suddenly everything is black. The next thing you know, you are in a dark cell.

"The Argonauts will never find you," Medea laughs from the other side of the door. "After my father kills your crew, he won't mind if I keep you for myself." Then she runs off.

You test the door, but it won't budge. You sag to the floor defeated. Sometime later in the night, the woman you carried across the river back on Mount Pelion enters your cell. "You!" you say, standing. "What are you doing here?"

Turn the page

"I came to make sure you are safe," she says.

"Are you really Hera?" you ask. "Can you help me escape?"

"I am," she says, sadly. "But I cannot. I asked Eros to shoot Medea with one of his arrows so that she would fall in love with you and help you. If you would have honored her devotion by marrying her, I would have seen you safely home. But since you refused her, it is she who will decide your fate."

Your fate is to spend the rest of your life imprisoned in King Aeetes' dungeon. Only Medea ever comes to visit you.

THE END

To follow another path, turn to page 13.

To learn more about Jason, turn to page 103.

You draw you sword and step in front of Medea to protect her. "Jason, don't," Medea says. "You can't …"

But it's too late to do anything else. The dragon rears its head. It hisses at you. Then in the blink of an eye, it lunges. You dive to the side, pulling Medea with you. "Get safely away," you tell Medea, and then you turn to the dragon.

Before it can strike again, you swing your sword at its long neck. CHING! Your blade bounces off the beast's scaly body. Your arm goes numb from the impact. Before you can recover, the dragon strikes again. This time you aren't quick enough to dive out of the way. It snatches you up in its mouth and devours you.

THE END

To follow another path, turn to page 13.

To learn more about Jason, turn to page 103.

You turn to Medea. "How can we defeat it?"

Medea steps in front of you and sings. Her voice is eerily beautiful.

Her song appears to affect the dragon. It sways back and forth. Its eyes blink shut. Then it collapses. "Did you kill it?" you ask.

"No," Medea gasps, out of breath. "It's just sleeping." Medea looks as if she's about to collapse herself, exhausted from the spell she just cast. "Be quick and get the fleece," she says.

You climb the hill and pull the Golden Fleece from the gnarled tree. "We need to be safely away before King Aeetes realizes that we took the Golden Fleece," you say once you're aboard the Argo. And then you begin your voyage home.

THE END

To follow another path, turn to page 13.

To learn more about Jason, turn to page 103.

CHAPTER 4

The Monsters

While your search for the Golden Fleece has been a success, you still need to reach home. Unknown dangers await you, and the king's fleet is now chasing you. Your ship, the Argo, is fast and sturdy. You have the witch, Medea, on your side. The winds favor you and fill your sails. But your crew is struggling, and King Aeetes is pursuing you for his Golden Fleece.

"Jason, we can't continue on like this," Orpheus says from the helm. "The men are exhausted." Orpheus is the world's greatest musician and one of the Argonauts, the group of heroes who joined you on your quest.

Turn the page.

Orpheus has been playing music to encourage the Argonauts. But you know what he said is true. You had to flee Colchis in the middle of the night, and no one has had time to rest.

As you're talking to Orpheus, Medea walks up to you. "What's wrong?" she asks.

"The crew," you explain. "They're exhausted, and I'm not sure how long they can keep this up."

"I know of another way home," Medea offers. "We can follow the river Ister to the Ionian Sea. My father won't follow because of the dangers."

You trust Medea. You escape her father's fleet. But in the Ionian Sea, you hear voices drifting over the water. In the distance you see a small island. "I wonder if they need help," one of your men, Butes, says.

To help the people on the island, go to page 83.
To keep sailing, turn to page 88.

Your crew members are among the greatest heroes of your day. You should see if you can help. You turn your ship toward the small island.

As you sail closer, the voices become clearer. They are beautiful. And then you hear their words. "Come brave sailor, so strong and bold."

As you listen, you watch your men stand up from their places at the oars. They start to crowd toward the bow of the ship. "Come brave sailor, be our hero."

Orpheus and Eribotes stand next to you. A look of concern crosses Orpheus' face. "Jason, don't listen to the voices," he says as he places one hand on your shoulder.

"But they need our help," Eribotes says on your other side.

To listen to the women, turn to page 84.

To listen to Orpheus, turn to page 86.

You knock Orpheus' hand aside. "They need our help," you say.

"But there's something wrong," he says. "I know it." You brush past Orpheus and knock his lute from his hands. You hear it crack as it hits the deck.

"I will save you!" you shout. Other men are climbing on the railings, about to jump into the water. You pull them back, shouting, "I am the captain! Me first!"

The men turn to you with a glint of anger in their eyes, but you don't notice it. Your focus is on the women and their beautiful song. You leap over the railing and dive into the water. One of the women on the island slides into the water and swims toward you. When she reaches you, she embraces you.

It's only when you're close to her that you realize she's not completely human. She has a long scaly tail instead of legs. Her smile is full of razor-sharp teeth. But none of this worries you. Her song continues to put you at ease, even as she drags you down to the ocean floor and your death.

THE END

To follow another path, turn to page 13.

To learn more about Jason, turn to page 103.

The women's song is clouding your thinking. You don't want to listen to what Orpheus is saying. You want only to help the women. But Orpheus has been a trusted member of your crew. If he says something's wrong, then something is wrong.

You see your men crowding against the rail. Eribotes climbs over and leaps into the water. Butes is about to follow. You turn to Orpheus. You are only able to mutter two words. "Do something," you say.

Orpheus stands above everyone else. He has his lute in hand.

"Listen to me, my brave Argonauts," he sings. "We have found what we sought." He sings louder and more beautifully than the women. As you watch, you see some of your men turn their heads toward him.

"Don't listen to that buffoon," the women sing. "For our song will make you swoon."

"Now our home calls us," Orpheus sings. "We must return to Iolcus." More and more men turn away from the women to listen to Orpheus.

"So grab your oars and row," Orpheus chants. "Row until the west winds blow."

Surprisingly the men do just as Orpheus sings. The Argo lurches forward.

We are moving! you think in amazement.

The farther away you move, the quieter the womens' song becomes and the less effect it has. Your men shake their heads and look around in confusion. If they had jumped into the water, your quest would have been doomed. But now your ship is sailing home again.

Turn to page 95.

You keep sailing and come to a narrow strait. On one side is a towering cliff wall. Its face is smooth, and you see several dark caves toward the top. On the other side is a rocky cliff face. The seas are rough along the cliff face, and you see a whirlpool swirling about at its base. "Do you know of these waters that we sail through?" you ask Medea.

"I do," she says. She points to the caves towering atop the towering cliff. "Scylla dwells up there. She has six doglike heads and is known to snatch up sailors from passing boats." Then she turns to the whirlpool and says, "And that is where Charybdis lives. He sucks ships down to the bottom of the ocean."

Both monsters are deadly, but you must face one of them to sail through the strait. Suddenly the water in front of your ship shoots upward.

The waterspout takes the form of a woman from the waist up. Your men gasp, but the goddess Hera has watched over you during your quest. Maybe she is sending you help.

"I am Thetis, one of the 50 Nereids," the water spirit says. "Hera has asked us to carry your ship to safety." Looking down into the water, you see the watery forms of the Nereids swimming around your boat. "But you must choose our path," Thetis says.

To travel under Scylla's lair, turn to page 90.

To travel over Charybdis' lair, turn to page 92.

You tell Thetis to go under Scylla's lair. She nods and then falls back into the water with a splash. You and your crew lean over the sides of the ship. Below you see the Nereids swim up to its hull. They lift your ship up onto their shoulders. Then they rise up as one so that they are out of the water from their waists up. The Argo is lifted completely out of the water.

The Nereids begin to swim forward. They stay clear of the whirlpool that marks Charybdis' lair and swim near the towering cliff where Scylla dwells. "We need to be on the alert," Medea warns. "Scylla could strike at any moment."

"To arms!" you shout to your men. They dash about grabbing swords and shields. You are almost past the dark caves when you see movement. A dark, hairy muzzle pokes out of one of the caves.

Turn to page 94.

You will brave Charybdis' lair. Thetis nods and then falls back into the water with a splash. You see the Nereids approach the ship. They set the Argo on their shoulders and raise it over the waves.

The Nereids swim away from the towering cliff where Scylla dwells. You breathe a sigh of relief. Charybdis is scary, but at least there aren't six heads to watch for.

As the Nereids near Charybdis' lair, the sea grows rough. The Nereids skirt around the edge of the whirlpool. A large mouth full of jagged teeth waits at the bottom of the whirlpool.

The pull of the whirlpool doesn't affect the Nereids, though. They continue walking across the water, carrying your ship past the dangers. Then they disappear beneath the waves.

Turn to page 95.

"There!" you shout, pointing. Your men are armed and ready. But you are still unprepared for the swiftness of Scylla's attack. A dog's head with a long neck darts out of one cave. It snatches up one of your men right in front of your eyes. You are too slow to react. Then another head attacks. And another. Three of your men are gone, and your crew is unable to stop Scylla.

Then you feel pain in your shoulder. Teeth dig into your flesh as you are lifted into the air. You scream and flail, but there's nothing you can do. You're quickly pulled into one of the dark caves and devoured.

THE END

To follow another path, turn to page 13.

To learn more about Jason, turn to page 103.

In the distance you see the island of Crete. It's just a dark speck among the waves. As you sail closer, the island spreads across the horizon. Crete is the largest of the many Greek islands that dot the Mediterranean.

As you sail closer, you spot the head and shoulders of a large, bronze statue poking above the nearby hills. "What is that?" you ask.

"That is Talos," Euphemus replies. "He guards the island from pirates."

You suddenly feel danger in the air. The bronze statue slowly turns its head toward you. Then he walks to the shore.

Turn the page.

Talos bends down and picks up a boulder. He tosses it into the air toward the Argo. It barely misses. You need to get out of the giant's range.

Talos reaches for another boulder. You grab a spear and start to head toward the stern of the Argo. But you feel a hand on your shoulder and stop. It's Medea. "I sense his weakness," she says. "There is a blood vessel on the back of his ankle."

"Do you know how to stop him?" you ask.

"I'm not sure," Medea replies.

To attack Talos with your spear, go to page 97.

To have Medea cast a spell, turn to page 99.

Another boulder splashes off the starboard. The waves it makes crash against the Argo's hull. The ship rocks. You stumble against the railing, nearly falling overboard.

As Talos bends down to pick up another boulder, you see the weak spot that Medea mentioned—a silver blood vessel along the back of its ankle.

"Stop rowing!" you shout to your crew as you rush toward the stern. You don't want the movement of the ship to ruin your aim.

With all your might, you hurl the spear. It sails through the air. Your aim is true. But just before it is about to strike Talos, the giant bats it away.

There isn't time to grab another spear as the giant hefts a rock over its head.

Turn the page.

Now that the Argo is motionless in the water, it makes for an easy target. When Talos launches the rock, it arcs through the air toward your ship. You turn to warn your men, but many of them have already leaped overboard.

The rock hits the ship and smashes through the deck with a loud CRACK! An explosion of wood sends splinters and planks whizzing through the air. You are thrown backward and smack your head against the mast. Your world goes black as the Argo begins to sink beneath the waves.

THE END

To follow another path, turn to page 13.

To learn more about Jason, turn to page 103.

"You have to try," you say to encourage Medea. She heads toward the stern of the boat. You follow. The next rock crashes to the port side of the Argo and sends waves crashing onto the deck. You help steady Medea as the ship rocks back and forth.

As the giant bends down to pick up another rock, Medea starts to sing. You can't understand her words, but they are filled with hate and anger. You aren't sure if her spell is working. But as Talos lifts up the next rock, he stumbles. The back of his leg brushes up against a cliff.

"Look!" Medea says, pointing at the giant's feet.

You look at the back of the giant's ankle and see molten lead leaking out. Talos cut himself on the rocky cliff. The giant's legs wobble.

Turn the page.

The giant leans to the right, then staggers to the left. Finally he falls forward, landing with a mighty thud on the beach. Your men cheer as you take up Medea in your arms and hug her. "You've saved us!" you shout.

As the Argo docks, several city guards march onto the docks. You meet them with Medea holding onto one arm and the Golden Fleece slung over the other. You can tell the guards are impressed. "Take me to my uncle," you say.

The guards lead you to the palace. They take you to the throne room and your uncle. He looks much older and more frail than when you had left on your quest. "I have succeeded in my quest," you proudly tell him. "I am here to reclaim the throne that my father once sat on."

THE END

To follow another path, turn to page 13.

To learn more about Jason, turn to page 103.

CHAPTER 5

A Tragic End

After completing the quests that they were renowned for, most Greek heroes did not lead happy lives. Perseus accidently killed his grandfather. Theseus was trapped in the Underworld for years. Although he was granted immortality, Hercules was poisoned by his second wife. Like the other heroes, Jason's life also ended tragically after his years of adventure.

King Pelias did not want to give up his throne. As revenge for his treatment of Jason, Medea plotted against the king.

Turn the page.

Pelias had grown old and feeble. Medea told his daughters that she knew of a way to make the king young again. But they would first have to cut up their father and place his remains in a pot. The daughters believed Medea and did as she said. But it was all a trick.

Once Pelias was dead, Jason became king. But not for long. The people of Iolcus were horrified by Pelias' death, and were terrified of Medea's magic. They drove the rulers out of the city.

The couple traveled to Corinth, where King Creon offered them a place to stay. The king also introduced Jason to his daughter, Glauce. King Creon offered his daughter's hand to Jason in marriage. Jason accepted, but first he had to divorce Medea. As revenge Medea sent Glauce a poisoned wedding dress, which killed Jason's future bride. When King Creon tried to save his daughter, he too was poisoned and died.

Medea fled Corinth and eventually ended up in Athens. She had a son named Medus with Athens' King Aegeus. Medea tried to trick King Aegeus into killing his oldest son so Medus could eventually become king. As punishment, Aegeus exiled her. Medea went back home to Colchis. There she helped her father regain the throne that he had lost after Jason stole the Golden Fleece.

Jason stayed in Corinth. Because he had broken his marriage vows to Medea, Hera no longer helped him. One day as an old man, he was sitting aboard the Argo and thinking back on his adventures. The ship was now old and creaky. It leaked and its wooden hull was rotting. Suddenly a beam fell from the mast and struck Jason, ending his life.

GODS AND GODDESSES

Athena—goddess of wisdom and protector of heroes. She was one of the ancient Greek's most important gods, as they valued wisdom above all else. In many Greek myths, Athena provided heroes with help to succeed on their quests. Athena was Zeus' daughter.

Boreas—the North Wind; he is seen as a winged, bearded man with a short, pleated tunic.

Eros—god of love. His bow and arrow can make people fall in love with the first person they see.

Hera—queen of the gods and goddess of marriage. She was married to Zeus. Hera was a jealous wife, as Zeus had many children with other goddesses and mortal women. Hera often thwarted Greek heroes who were Zeus' sons.

Iris—messenger to the gods. She carries a staff and a vase and is the human form of a rainbow.

Poseidon—the god of the seas and Zeus' brother. Poseidon is known for his temper. He is often shown holding a trident. When he gets mad, Poseidon slams his trident on the groud to cause an earthquake.

Zeus—god of the sky and ruler of the Greek gods. Zeus was also the father of many of the most famous Greek heroes, such as Hercules and Perseus. His weapon was a thunderbolt.

OTHER PATHS TO EXPLORE

During his quest for the Golden Fleece, Jason faced many dangers. You have read about some of his most well-known stories, including aiding King Phineus, yoking King Aeetes' fire breathing bulls, and facing Scylla and Charybdis. But some of these adventures might have had different endings if Jason had acted differently.

1. When Jason first left Iolcus, Hercules was part of his crew. Hercules was the strongest man alive and half god. But after his friend Hylas went missing, Hercules did not want to continue on with Jason's quest. Calais and Zetes convinced Jason to leave Hercules behind. How do you think Jason would have chased off the Harpies if Hercules had helped him instead of Calais and Zetes? (Integration of Knowledge and Ideas)

2. Medea's magic helped Jason yoke King Aeetes' fire-breathing bulls. It also put the dragon that guarded the Golden Fleece to sleep. How do you think Jason could have succeeded against these monsters without Medea's help? (Integration of Knowledge and Ideas)

3. Shortly after leaving Iolcus, Jason landed on an unknown land. He went searching for supplies with some of his men. They were attacked by the Earthborn. These giants rose up out of the ground and hurled rocks at Jason's crew. How do you think Jason and his men were able to defeat the monsters made out of earth? (Integration of Knowledge and Ideas)

GLOSSARY

Argonauts (AR-guh-NAHTS)—the heroes who accompanied Jason on his quest; their name comes from Jason's ship, the Argos.

blood vessel (BLUHD VE-suhl)—a tube that caries blood through your body; arteries and veins are blood vessels.

centaur (SEN-tor)—a creature with the head and chest of a human and the body of a horse

fleet (FLEET)—a group of warships under one command

frail (FRAY-uhl)—weak or delicate

harpy (HARP-ee)—a mythological creature believed to have a woman's head and the wings and body of a bird

hull (HUHL)—the main body or casing of a hovercraft, boat, ship, tank, or tanklike armored vehicle

lute (LUHT)—a stringed instrument with a neck and a deep round back

Nereids (NEER-ee-ihds)—female sea spirits or sea nymphs; the Nereids came to the aid of men who needed help.

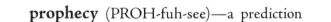

prophecy (PROH-fuh-see)—a prediction

starboard (STAR-burd)—the right-hand side of a ship

strait (STRAYT)—a narrow waterway connecting two large bodies of water

whirlpool (WURL-pool)—a water current that moves rapidly in a circle; ships and boats can become caught in whirlpools.

yoke (YOKE)—a wooden frame attached to the necks of work animals; a yoke links two animals together for plowing.

Read More

Jeffrey, Gary. *Jason and the Argonauts.* New York: Gareth Stevens Pub., 2013.

Nicolaides, Selene. *Gods, Heroes, and Monsters.* Hauppauge, N.Y.: Barrons Educations Series, Inc., 2016.

Smith, Neil. *Jason and the Argonauts.* New York: Rosen Publishing, 2015.

Internet Sites

FactHound offers a safe, fun way to find Internet sites related to this book. All of the sites on FactHound have been researched by our staff.

Here's all you do:
Visit *www.facthound.com*
Type in this code: 9781491481134

BIBLIOGRAPHY

Barnett, Mary. *Gods and Myths of Ancient Greece.* New York: Modern Publishing Regency House, 1997.

Buxton, Richard. *The Complete World of Greek Mythology.* London: Thames & Hudson, Ltd., 2004.

Freeman, Philip. *Oh My Gods: A Modern Retelling of Greek and Roman Myths.* New York: Simon & Schuster, 2012.

Moncrieff, A. R. Hope. *Myths and Legends of Ancient Greece.* New York: Gramercy Books, 1995.

Ovid (trans. Mary M. Innes). *Metamorphoses.* New York: Penguin Books, 1955.

Stapleton, Michael. *The Illustrated Dictionary of Greek and Roman Mythology.* New York: Peter Bedrick Books, 1986.

Waterfield, Robin. *The Greek Myths: Stories of the Greek Gods and Heroes Vividly Retold.* New York: Metro Books, 2011.

Watts, Christopher, "Why Did the Greeks Tell Myths?" academia.edu, 2010, http://www.academia.edu/2922375/Why_ did_the_Greeks_tell_Myths_Perseus (April 4, 2015).

INDEX